S0-AZQ-130

Christmas Love Letters from God

Bible Stories

Written by
Glenys Nellist

Illustrated by
Rachel Clowes

ZONDERkidz

This book is dedicated to Isabel Hughes,
who went to heaven far too early.

Thank you Mum, for making Christmas
a magical time for me.
—G.N.

For Dad and Mum
—R.C.

ZONDERKIDZ

Christmas Love Letters from God
Copyright © 2016 by Glenys Nellist
Illustrations © 2016 by Rachel Clowes

This title is also available as a Zondervan ebook. Visit www.zondervan.com/ebooks.

Requests for information should be addressed to:

Zonderkidz, 3900 Sparks Dr. SE, Grand Rapids, Michigan 49546

ISBN 978-0-310-74824-3

All Scripture quotations, unless otherwise indicated, are taken from The Holy Bible, *New International Reader's Version®, NIrV®*. Copyright © 1995, 1996, 1998, 2014 by Biblica, Inc.® Used by permission of Zondervan. All rights reserved worldwide. www.zondervan.com. The "NIrV" and "New International Reader's Version" are trademarks registered in the United States Patent and Trademark Office by Biblica, Inc.®

Any Internet addresses (websites, blogs, etc.) and telephone numbers in this book are offered as a resource. They are not intended in any way to be or imply an endorsement by Zondervan, nor does Zondervan vouch for the content of these sites and numbers for the life of this book.

All rights reserved. No part of this publication may be reproduced, stored in a retrieval system, or transmitted in any form or by any means—electronic, mechanical, photocopy, recording, or any other—except for brief quotations in printed reviews, without the prior permission of the publisher.

Zonderkidz is a trademark of Zondervan.

Art direction and design: Jody Langley

Printed in China

16 17 18 19 20 21 /LPC/ 22 21 20 19 18 17 16 15 14 13 12 11 10 9 8 7 6 5 4 3 2 1

Stories

Isaiah's Good News

Isaiah 9:2; 6–7

It was hundreds and hundreds of years before Jesus was born. Isaiah was lying in bed thinking about God. It was his favorite thing to do. Isaiah loved God. He loved it when God spoke to him and gave him a message for the people. It made him feel special to be God's messenger.

Isaiah was wondering what message God would give him next when he saw something amazing. A huge light was shining in the darkness. And the light was so big and so bright and so beautiful that nothing could put it out. Was Isaiah dreaming? No—he was not asleep. This wonderful light was real. It was God's message—a message of good news for the people. A very special baby was going to be born—a baby who would bring light to the whole world. Isaiah was so excited he threw his blanket on the floor and jumped out of bed. He ran outside into the streets and hopped, skipped, clapped, and shouted to anyone who would listen:

My friends, I have to tell you, that I have seen the light!
He is coming to the darkness. He will chase away the night.
Although he will be little, he'll be super, super strong.
He will grow into a King. He will teach us right from wrong.
His name will last forever, Prince of Peace, the Mighty One.
He'll be Father to the world, but he'll also be a Son.
And he'll sit upon his throne with his light for all to see.
He will rescue us from darkness, and the world will be set free.

Isaiah knew the wonderful light would come—but he didn't know when or how or who the baby would be. Only God knew.

God's Perfect Promise

I am the light of the world.
John 8:12

*Your Love Letter
from God*

Mary's Song

Luke 1:26–38; 46–50

In her little home in Nazareth, Mary had just finished sweeping the floor when she heard a strange noise behind her. It sounded like a rustling in the air, a whispering of silvery wings. Mary turned around and nearly fainted in fear. There, right in front of her, stood a beautiful angel. "Hello, Mary," the angel said softly. "God is with you."

Mary was terrified, but the angel smiled and said, "Don't be afraid. God has chosen you to be the mother of his Son."

"But how can that be?" Mary cried. "I'm not married."

"Don't worry," the angel replied. "Trust God. You must name your little boy Jesus. He will be King of the whole world."

Mary listened in wonder to the angel's words. Could it be true? Was she really going to have a baby? Would he be a King? Mary's heart filled with joy and she bowed her head and whispered, "I'm ready, God."

As the angel Gabriel flew back to heaven, Mary closed her eyes and began to sing softly.

Oh my soul, my heart is singing,
And my spirit fills with joy,
For I will be the momma
Of a precious baby boy.
And God will be the papa
Of that special baby Son.
All the people will remember
What the Mighty One has done.

As Mary sang, her words floated up into heaven. When God heard them, he smiled. And when Mary opened her eyes, the sun was shining—streaming straight through her window. To Mary it felt like God's warm and wonderful blessings were falling on her, covering her from the top of her head to the tips of her toes. And they were.

Your Love Letter
from God

God's Perfect Promise
The light of my blessing will
shine on you.
Isaiah 58:8

Joseph's Dream

Matthew 1:18–24

Joseph could not sleep. He tossed and turned in bed. Was his pillow too hard? No, it was not his pillow keeping him awake. It was something he had heard about Mary. Mary was the only girl Joseph loved, the one he had promised to marry. But how could he marry her now? Mary was going to have a baby, and that baby would be God's Son! How could that possibly be? Who had ever heard of such a thing? Joseph closed his eyes. As he drifted off to sleep, he heard the voice of an angel, singing softly into the darkness.

Joseph, son of David, what Mary says is true,
But please don't be afraid. God will show you what to do.
You need to be with Mary—the only girl you love,
Because she has been chosen, chosen from above.
She's going to have a baby. He **really** is God's Son.
You must name him Jesus—he will be the Chosen One.
He needs someone to love him, to watch him learn and grow.
Will you help be his daddy? God really needs to know.

When Joseph woke up, the air in the room seemed to dance and glitter in the early morning sun. And Joseph knelt by his bed and said yes to God.

God's Perfect Promise

I will make you strong
and help you.
Isaiah 41:10

Your Love Letter
from God

Bethlehem's Road

Luke 2:1–5

Mary put her hand on her tummy as she finished packing her bags for the journey ahead. It wasn't long now before her little boy would be born. But before he came, she had to travel all the way to Bethlehem with Joseph. Seventy miles! That was such a long way. But Mary and Joseph had no choice. They had to go back to their hometown to be counted.

Mary packed some bread for the journey while Joseph draped a blanket over the donkey's back. "Are you ready, Mary?" Joseph called.

Mary pulled her shawl over her head as Joseph helped her climb onto the little donkey. "I'm ready, Joseph," she said.

As Joseph took the donkey's reins, Mary took one last look at the home she was leaving in Nazareth. She did not know what might happen in Bethlehem. But no matter what, Mary was ready. She knew Joseph would take care of her, and God would take care of her baby. And so Mary and Joseph set off on Bethlehem's road.

Traveling through the nighttime, traveling through the day,
A donkey carried Mary, all along the way.
Up and down the hillsides, over rock and sand,
Joseph walked beside her, holding Mary's hand.
Through the woods and valleys, until they saw the sight,
A little town called Bethlehem, where they would spend the night.
What would happen in this place? Mary did not know.
She only knew that where she went, God was sure to go.

By the time Mary and Joseph reached the little town of Bethlehem, every inn was full. The only room for them was a small stable. Mary was so tired she curled up in the soft hay and fell fast asleep. Joseph covered her with his cloak as darkness and quiet fell all around. Even though it was quiet, Joseph knew they weren't alone. God was there. God was in the quiet, and God was in the darkness, waiting … waiting for his Son to be born.

Your Love Letter
from God

God's Perfect Promise
I will march out ahead of you.
Isaiah 45:2

Jesus Joy!

Luke 2:6–7

Mary hadn't been asleep very long when she suddenly woke up. Even though it was the middle of the night, the darkness had gone. A huge star was peeping in through the window of the little stable. In its light Mary could see the cows and sheep curled up in the soft hay. Mary sat up. She shook Joseph by the shoulder. "Wake up, Joseph!" she cried. "It's time for our baby to be born." Joseph jumped up and rubbed his eyes. He saw the bright star shining in through the window. "This is what we've been waiting for, Mary," Joseph whispered. It was time to welcome Jesus into the world.

In a little stable, in the middle of the night,
While all the cows lay sleeping and a star was shining bright,
A child was born to Mary, a brand-new baby boy,
The bells rang out in heaven, and the angels danced for joy!
Baby Jesus had been born. A Savior—God's own Son.
A Christmas gift from heaven, God sent for everyone.
Mary cuddled Jesus and she whispered in his ear,
"Welcome to the world, my love. We're so glad you're here."

Mary wrapped her newborn baby in strips of cloth, while Joseph made a warm, comfy bed for him in the manger. And baby Jesus closed his eyes and went straight to sleep.

Your Love Letter
from God

God's Perfect Promise

A Savior has been born to you.

Luke 2:11

Shepherd's Surprise

Luke 2:8–20

A big, round, yellow moon shone bright over Bethlehem's fields. Sheep lay sleeping, with their little lambs snuggled close by their side. Shepherds dozed, huddled together for warmth. All was quiet and still. But somewhere, in the distance, music began to float over the hills—a song that got louder and louder as it danced in the air. The shepherds opened their eyes and couldn't believe what they saw. It was an angel! The shepherds were terrified. They clutched their cloaks around them in fear. But the angel smiled and spoke to them.

"Shepherds, do not worry! No need to be upset!
For I bring you good news—and no one knows it yet.
A baby has been born. He is Jesus, God's own Son,
And you must go and see him. Then tell everyone!
He is lying fast asleep, in a stable not too far.
You will know just how to find it—it's the one under the star."
And as the shepherds hurried, a choir of angels sang,
"Glory, Alleluia, to the King of all the land!"

When the shepherds arrived at the stable, it was just as the angel had told them. There was the tiny baby King, lying fast asleep in a manger. What a wonderful surprise! The shepherds clapped their hands, the sheep *baaed* loudly, and the baby lambs skipped around the stable. The shepherds were so excited they told everyone they saw what had happened. It was a night they would never, ever forget.

God's Perfect Promise
I will tell you great things.
Jeremiah 33:3

Your Love Letter
from God

Wise Men's Wonder

Matthew 2:1–11

In a country far, far away from Bethlehem, three wise men were looking up into the dark, night sky. They loved to watch and study the stars as they twinkled overhead. But tonight, there was a brand-new star! It was bigger, and brighter, and far more beautiful than any star they had ever seen before. Such an important star could only mean one thing— the King had been born! "Let's go!" they cried. The three wise men picked out their finest gifts, jumped on their camels, and set off across the desert.

"Let's go find the baby! Let's go find the King!
Let's take him lots of treasures—our finest gifts we'll bring."
The camels plodded onwards, over many, many miles,
The wise men were so tired—but they had to see the child!
Though the journey was not easy, after many, many nights,
They saw the bright star shining—what a happy, happy sight!
They jumped down from their camels, and they bowed before the boy.
They had found the one they searched for—and their hearts were filled with joy.

The three wise men knelt down in front of Jesus. They gave him their gifts of gold, frankincense, and myrrh. All the miles they had traveled; all those hot days and nights in the desert; all that bouncing up and down on their camels; every single bit of their hard journey had been worth it. They had found the one they searched for; the one they believed in; they had found Jesus—King of the whole world.